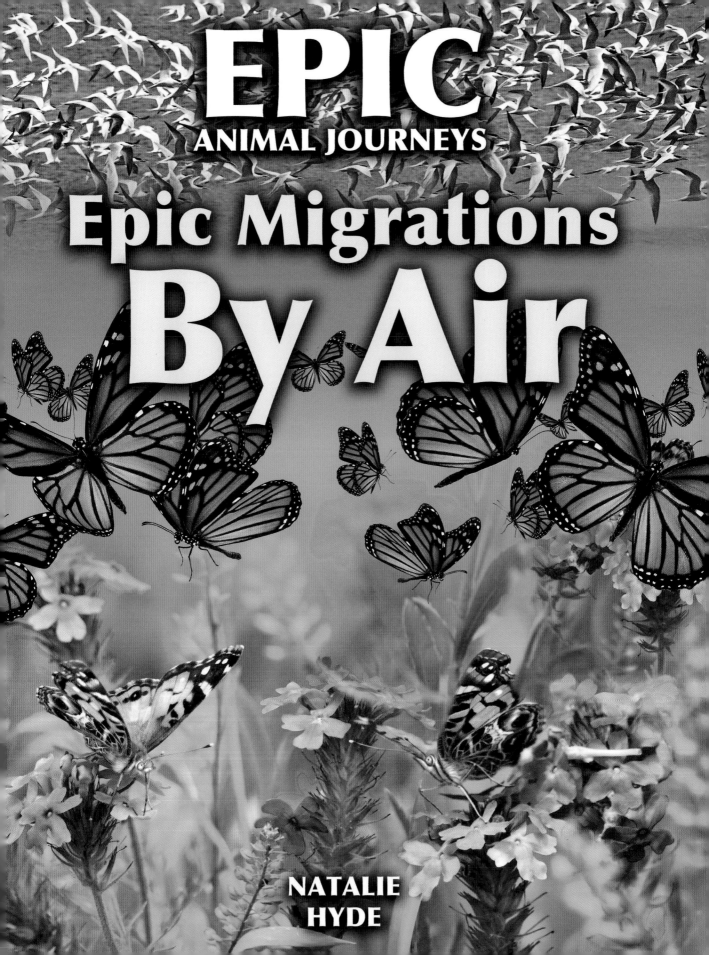

EPIC
ANIMAL JOURNEYS

Epic Migrations
By Air

NATALIE
HYDE

CRABTREE
PUBLISHING COMPANY
WWW.CRABTREEBOOKS.COM

Author:
Natalie Hyde
Series research and development:
Reagan Miller, Janine Deschenes
Editorial director:
Kathy Middleton
Editors:
Sonya Newland, Ellen Rodger
Proofreaders:
Izzi Howell, Melissa Boyce
Graphic design:
White-Thomson Publishing
Katherine Berti
Image research:
Natalie Hyde
Print and production coordinator:
Katherine Berti

Images:

Alamy
Chocoholic p. 11b; BIOSPHOTO
p. 17b; Jamie Roach p. 29r

iStock
milehightraveler p. 3, 20t; Antenore
p. 5b; drbimages p. 9b; ehughes
p. 9 inset; emkaplin p. 10; Stefan
Rotter p. 17t; membio p. 18b;
KeithSzafranski p. 21t; ehughes
p. 31

All other images by Shutterstock

Contents page: Whooping crane in flight

Library and Archives Canada Cataloguing in Publication

Title: Epic migrations by air / Natalie Hyde.
Names: Hyde, Natalie, 1963- author.
Description: Series statement: Epic animal journeys | Includes index.
Identifiers: Canadiana (print) 20190098015 |
  Canadiana (ebook) 20190098023 |
  ISBN 9780778763673 (hardcover) |
  ISBN 9780778763710 (softcover) |
  ISBN 9781427123480 (HTML)
Subjects: LCSH: Animal migration—Juvenile literature. |
  LCSH: Nature—Effect of human beings on—Juvenile literature.
Classification: LCC QL754 .H93 2019 | DDC j591.56/8—dc23

Library of Congress Cataloging-in-Publication Data

Names: Hyde, Natalie, 1963- author.
Title: Epic migrations by air / Natalie Hyde.
Description: New York, New York : Crabtree Publishing Company, [2019] |
  Series: Epic animal journeys | Includes index.
Identifiers: LCCN 2019015754 (print) | LCCN 2019017766 (ebook) |
  ISBN 9780778763673 (hardcover) |
  ISBN 9780778763710 (pbk.) |
  ISBN 9781427123480 (ebook)
Subjects: LCSH: Animal migration--Juvenile literature. | Nature--Effect of
  human beings on--Juvenile literature.
Classification: LCC QL754 .H9425 2019 (print) | LCC QL754 (ebook) |
  DDC 591.56/8--dc23
LC record available at https://lccn.loc.gov/2019015754
LC ebook record available at https://lccn.loc.gov/2019017766

Crabtree Publishing Company

www.crabtreebooks.com   1-800-387-7650

Printed in the U.S.A./082019/CG20190712

**Published
in Canada
Crabtree Publishing**
616 Welland Ave.
St. Catharines, Ontario
L2M 5V6

**Published in the
United States
Crabtree Publishing**
PMB 59051
350 Fifth Avenue, 59th Floor
New York, New York 10118

**Published in the
United Kingdom
Crabtree Publishing**
Maritime House
Basin Road North, Hove
BN41 1WR

**Published
in Australia
Crabtree Publishing**
Unit 3 – 5 Currumbin Court
Capalaba
QLD 4157

Contents

Air Migrations

Painted lady butterflies make a 9,000-mile (14,480 km) round trip annually.

On Their Way

Animals do not always stay in one place for the whole year. Some make a regular, long journey called a migration. Some travel to find better sources of food and water. Others migrate in search of cooler or warmer weather when the seasons change. Some head to areas that are safer for mating or having young. Animals that fly use winds and air currents to travel long distances.

Painted lady butterflies seek warmer weather when they migrate from Europe to Africa. They can fly up to 62 miles (100 km) in a day. They arrive just as their favorite flowers bloom so they can feed on the nectar. Bogong moths in Australia migrate to cooler caves in the southeast mountains when the temperature gets too hot farther north.

Bat Nursery

Mexican free-tailed bats migrate to find safer conditions to raise their young. They leave Mexico in February and head to Texas. The males group together while the females create large **maternity wards**. The caves they live in offer the baby bats the warmth and safety they need to grow. In October, the entire colony heads back to large caves in northern and central Mexico.

Mexican free-tailed bats need certain conditions for their young. The caves have to be warm and humid—and big enough for a large colony!

Spectacular Swallows

Animals have followed particular migration routes for thousands of years. Sometimes they head to the same stream, cave, or even tree, year after year. Each year around March 19, cliff swallows return to the eaves of the same building, the Mission, in San Juan Capistrano, California.

Cliff swallows spend the summer nesting in the eaves of the Mission in San Juan Capistrano. Toward the end of October, they set off on the 6,000-mile (9,656 km) flight south to Argentina.

5

Time to Go

Scientists are still not certain what triggers animals to start migrating each year. It might be a combination of factors. Days getting shorter and temperatures getting colder can signal that winter is coming. Their food supply can change as prey hibernate or plants die out. Sometimes migration might be instinctive—an inborn need to perform a behavior.

Arctic terns fly in a zigzag pattern when they migrate. This lets them follow huge spiraling wind patterns. That way, they can glide most of the way and save their energy.

Follow Me

Migrating animals find their way year after year. This is pretty amazing, because the landscape is always changing and sometimes there are no adults to show young animals the way. Scientists think that many birds follow magnetic lines that circle Earth. Mountains and rivers serve as landmarks. But not all migrating animals follow the same route each time. They sometimes change their path to follow a food source or wind currents.

Getting In the Way

Human activity can disturb migratory routes. For animals that migrate by air, this means tall buildings, radio towers, wind turbines, and power lines may cause them to crash and die.

Human activity can also damage areas where migrating birds rest and feed. Cutting down trees and building houses can leave the birds with no protected areas to roost. **Pesticides** and oil spills can poison their food. **Climate change** is causing water sources to dry up. Groups such as BirdLife International are trying to work with governments to protect these areas.

Between 140,000 and 328,000 birds are killed by wind turbine blades in the U.S. each year. The higher the turbine, the more deaths there are.

Monarch Butterfly

Habitat	Southern Canada to northern South America and California
Known for	A four- or five-**generation** migration
When	Fall through spring

Monarch butterflies typically live for two to six weeks. However, the migrating generation lives for up to seven months through the fall and winter to make the long trip south.

North America

N

Canada

United States

Rocky Mountains

Appalachian Mountains

Atlantic Ocean

Mexico

Pacific Ocean

Gulf of Mexico

Monarch Butterfly Migration

→ *Migration routes*

⬭ *Late summer range*

 Winter roosts

The Journey

The migration begins in Canada, in late August. Monarchs that hatch in August or September do not **reproduce**. Instead, they store fat to help them survive their migration. Then they begin their 1,864-mile (3,000 km) journey. Monarchs ride rising columns of air to save energy. This means they don't need to flap their wings as often. At night and in bad weather they rest in trees.

Monarchs usually reach their wintering sites by the end of October. The eastern population arrives in Mexico.

The butterflies group together in small areas, filling the fir trees. The population west of the Rocky Mountains heads to Pacific Grove, California, and rests in eucalyptus trees.

In the spring, monarchs head north with the warm weather. Females lay eggs along the way. As the new generation hatches, they continue north. This happens three or four times. By the time the monarchs reach Canada again, they are the fourth or fifth generation of the butterflies that first flew south.

Along their journey, monarchs feed on nectar from flowers such as lilac and goldenrod.

*Monarch **roosts** may have so many butterflies that the branches bend with the weight.*

Knowing the Way

For hundreds of years, no one knew where monarchs went when they migrated. In the 1940s, Dr. Fred Urquhart from the University of Toronto began tagging these butterflies. This later revealed that monarchs spent the winters in the cool mountains of central Mexico. Scientists still don't understand how different butterflies return to the same trees. They believe it might be a kind of **genetic memory**.

Natural Obstacles

Monarchs face many dangers during their short lifetime. Diseases may make them too weak to complete the migration. Mice and some birds feed on them. Even when they reach their winter roosts, they still face danger. Winter storms in Mexico have sometimes killed up to 90 percent of the monarchs.

Tags on the butterflies give scientists information about the pace of the migration as well as where the monarchs that reach Mexico come from.

Human Roadblocks

Monarch caterpillars only eat milkweed. Pesticides used to kill milkweed plants near crops stop monarchs from laying eggs for a new generation. This loss of habitat is disastrous. In Mexico, logging or clearing the forest for farming leaves monarchs without any protection from **predators** or the weather over the winter.

Monarch butterflies lay their eggs on milkweed leaves so that as soon as the caterpillars hatch, they can start eating.

Positive Human Efforts

The number of monarchs is decreasing every year. Project Milkweed is helping people find milkweed seeds so they can plant this helpful wildflower for monarch caterpillars. The organization Monarch Watch encourages everyone to create monarch way stations in gardens, schools, parks, and zoos. Way stations include milkweed plants, nectar plants, and water sources.

MONARCH WAYSTATION

This site provides milkweeds, nectar sources, and shelter needed to sustain monarch butterflies as they migrate through North America.
Certified and registered by Monarch Watch as an official Monarch Waystation.
CREATE, CONSERVE, & PROTECT MONARCH HABITATS

WWW.MONARCHWATCH.ORG
Monarch Watch • University of Kansas • Entomology Program • 1200 Sunnyside Ave. • Lawrence, KS 66045-7534

Monarch way stations can provide the butterflies with food, water, and shelter as they migrate.

Bar-tailed Godwit

Habitat	Alaska, East Asia, Europe, Australia, Africa, and New Zealand
Known for	The longest known nonstop migration
When	September, October, and March

Bar-tailed godwits breed in the high Arctic. They take different migration routes to four main overwintering sites.

N

Alaska

Europe

Asia

Pacific Ocean

Africa

Atlantic Ocean

Bar-tailed Godwit Migration

→ Two-way migration routes

● Summer breeding grounds

● Wintering grounds

Australia

New Zealand

The Journey

Bar-tailed godwits breed in open, marshy **tundra** in late May and August. After the eggs hatch, the birds move to the coastline to feed and grow. They eat insects, worms, mollusks, seeds, and berries to build up their fat stores. This gives them energy for the migration. When they begin to migrate, they are about twice the size they were when they were breeding! They need the extra fuel to make the epic flight.

Some groups of godwits spend the summers in Scandinavia or northern Russia. These birds fly mostly over land to their winter grounds in West Africa or the coast of the Indian Ocean. But the groups in Siberia or Alaska have long stretches over water, where it is not easy to feed or rest. These birds make the longest migration by air of any animal.

One tagged godwit flew nonstop to New Zealand from Alaska. This was a new flight record of 7,258 miles (11,680 km). The journey took around 175 hours.

About 70,000 bar-tailed godwits make the journey from New Zealand to Alaska and back each year.

13

Knowing the Way

Banding is a way of tracking migratory birds by putting a small metal or plastic tag on their leg. This helps scientists follow their movements. Some godwits have been recaptured more than 18 years after they were first banded. A godwit can travel over 126,000 miles (203,000 km) in a lifetime.

The Changing Climate

If there is not a good food supply in the Arctic, godwits will not have enough fat stored to make the long flight. Climate change and a warming Arctic have affected the number and health of the plants and insects that godwits feed on. Rising sea levels are taking over their nesting areas on the shoreline. Climate change may also be affecting wind patterns. This is a problem for godwits, because they use winds to save energy in flight.

Young godwits make their first migration when they are barely four months old.

Human Roadblocks

One group of godwits migrates in two stages. They fly from northern Russia to the Yellow Sea and then on to South Asia and Australia. Habitat loss in the Yellow Sea has affected the godwits that stop here to rest and feed before continuing their journey.

Godwits are usually silent while on the ground. Just before they migrate and while in flight they make their "a-wik, a-wik, a-wik" call.

> *The Maori people of New Zealand traditionally believe godwits accompany the spirits of the dead.*

Habitat Protection

The bar-tailed godwit is listed with the African-Eurasian Waterbird Agreement (AEWA). This is an international treaty designed to protect birds that live in wetland habitats. New Zealand is the winter home of a large number of godwits. The country is a member of the East Asian-Australasian Flyway Partnership (EAAFP). This group works with governments to protect key habitats along the flyways of migratory birds.

Marmalade Hoverfly

Habitat	Europe, northern Asia, and northern Africa
Known for	Its **beneficial** migration
When	Spring and fall

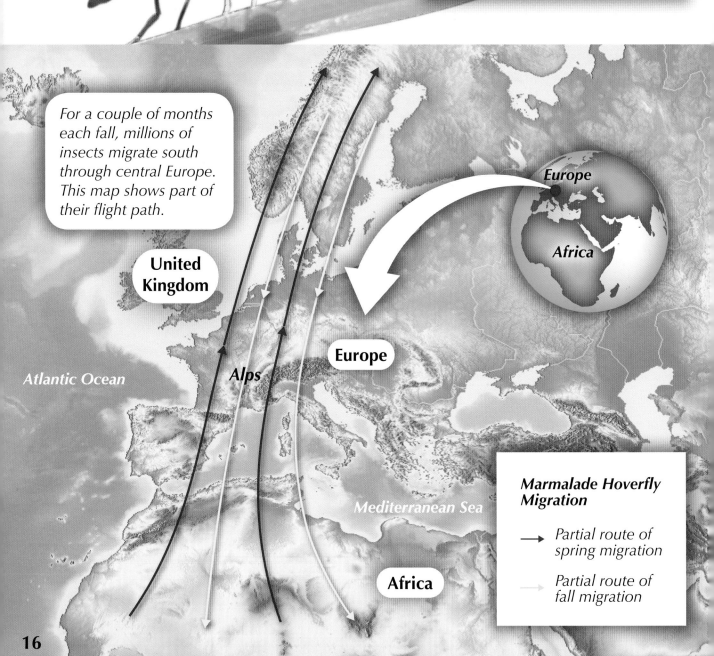

For a couple of months each fall, millions of insects migrate south through central Europe. This map shows part of their flight path.

Europe

Africa

United Kingdom

Europe

Atlantic Ocean

Alps

Mediterranean Sea

Africa

Marmalade Hoverfly Migration

→ Partial route of spring migration

→ Partial route of fall migration

The Journey

Hoverfly **larvae** feed on aphids. Aphids are tiny green insects that suck the sap out of plants, weakening them. They damage crops and carry viruses that infect the plants. The hoverfly migration follows outbreaks of aphids. Hoverflies lay their eggs in aphid colonies. After a couple of weeks, the eggs hatch and the hoverfly larvae feast on the aphids.

Heading North

Hoverflies spend the winter in southern Europe and northern Africa. There, rain causes plants to bloom and aphids to multiply. As spring arrives and rainfall decreases, hoverflies head north. They may fly over 62 miles (100 km) a day, using wind currents to help them along. They arrive in Europe and the U.K. by summer.

Adult hoverflies move from flower to flower, sipping nectar. This **pollinates** the flowers and helps them reproduce. Marmalade hoverflies live only a few weeks. When cold weather returns, the new generation of hoverflies migrates south again.

The marmalade hoverfly gets its name from the orange color between the black bands on its body.

hoverfly larva

aphid

It only takes about two hoverfly larvae to control a whole colony of aphids.

Hoverflies get their name from their ability to hover, especially when sipping nectar.

Mass Movement

Marmalade hoverflies often migrate in swarms of thousands or even millions. They may be seen migrating with other insects, such as admiral butterflies and dragonflies. Sometimes when the insects land, they are so thick that they pile up in drifts.

Climate Change

Marmalade hoverflies have stripes on their abdomen. This is a kind of **camouflage** because it makes them look like wasps. But this means that people sometimes kill them out of fear. Climate change is another problem for the marmalade hoverfly. Unexpected cold or hot weather can kill the plants they feed on. Extreme storms can make their migration difficult or impossible.

One way to tell marmalade hoverflies from wasps is their wings. Wasps have four wings while hoverflies have only two.

Human Roadblocks

Pesticides that kill aphids on crops rob marmalade hoverfly larvae of their food. Also, growing cities lead to loss of habitat for hoverflies. Without plants to host aphids, hoverflies will have nowhere to lay their eggs. Fewer hoverflies means less pollination for plants.

Taking Action

Charities such as the Wildlife Trusts recognize the importance of hoverflies. They urge people to include gardens in their outdoor spaces. They suggest planting flowers that hoverflies need for food. Studies have shown the link between pest control and the decrease in hoverflies. Organizations such as Pesticide Action Network (PAN) are campaigning to limit the use of chemicals that kill beneficial insects.

Hoverflies find yellow flowers with bright yellow pollen attractive because they are a good food source.

Whooping Crane

Habitat	Alberta, Northwest Territories, Wisconsin, Texas, Florida
Known for	"Operation Migration"
When	Spring and fall

During their long journey south, cranes fly over hundreds of utility lines. Researchers have developed new ways of marking the lines so the birds can see and avoid them.

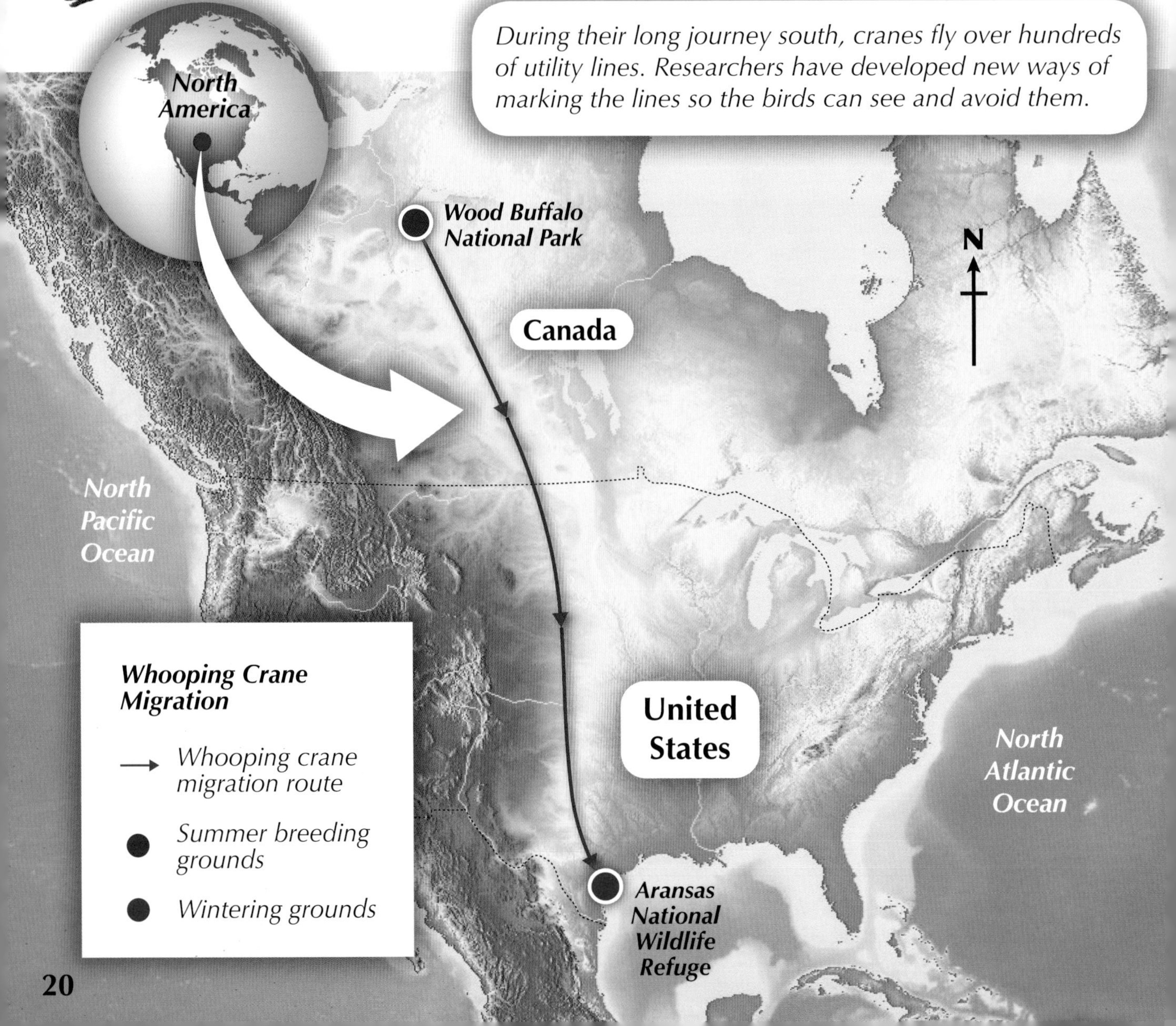

North America

N

Wood Buffalo National Park

Canada

North Pacific Ocean

United States

North Atlantic Ocean

Whooping Crane Migration

→ Whooping crane migration route

● Summer breeding grounds

● Wintering grounds

Aransas National Wildlife Refuge

Migrating whooping cranes often feed with sandhill cranes in fields of harvested crops.

The Journey

The only wild whooping crane flock spends its summers in Wood Buffalo National Park, in Alberta and the Northwest Territories, Canada. The birds nest and raise their young there. Around October, they begin the long journey to their wintering grounds. They travel about 2,500 miles (4,025 km). They stop briefly at wetlands along the way to rest and feed.

Whooping cranes do not usually migrate in large groups. Often, two or three birds travel together. As the population of whooping cranes grows, it is likely that migrating groups will also get bigger. Their usual winter grounds are the Aransas National Wildlife Refuge in Texas. Researchers have noticed that the whooping cranes are now exploring new areas to overwinter.

Whooping cranes fly with their long legs out behind them.

Operation Migration

With only one wild flock, conservationists decided to create new flocks in Florida and Wisconsin. In 2001, eggs taken from nests in the Northwest Territories were hatched in **incubators**. Ultralight aircraft were used to stand in for adult birds. Researchers prepared the chicks by playing the sound of ultralight engines before they even hatched. They exposed them to ultralights at a few days old. They played whooping crane calls from the plane and the chicks followed it on the ground. Finally, they learned to fly behind it.

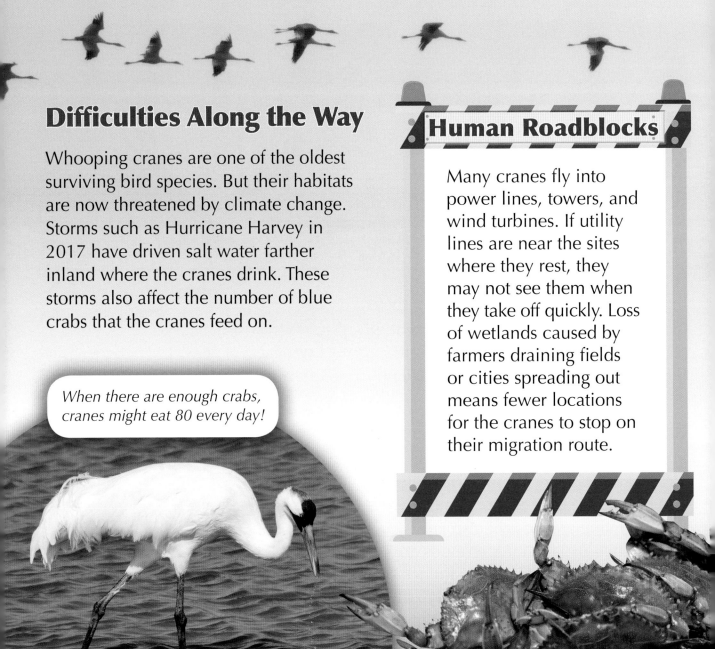

Difficulties Along the Way

Whooping cranes are one of the oldest surviving bird species. But their habitats are now threatened by climate change. Storms such as Hurricane Harvey in 2017 have driven salt water farther inland where the cranes drink. These storms also affect the number of blue crabs that the cranes feed on.

When there are enough crabs, cranes might eat 80 every day!

Human Roadblocks

Many cranes fly into power lines, towers, and wind turbines. If utility lines are near the sites where they rest, they may not see them when they take off quickly. Loss of wetlands caused by farmers draining fields or cities spreading out means fewer locations for the cranes to stop on their migration route.

Watching Out for Whoopers

Whooper Watch is a program that encourages U.S. citizens to watch for migrating whooping cranes. The public can report sightings to help keep the area quiet while the migrating birds rest. The International Crane Foundation works to protect crane water sources, flyways, and nesting grounds.

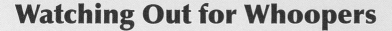

Operation Migration ended in 2018, but more than 100 whooping cranes now migrate on their own from Wisconsin to Florida.

In 1941, there were only 16 whooping cranes left in the wild. Today, there are over 300. Groups helping with their conservation know it is slow but steady progress.

Canada Goose

Habitat	Native to arctic North America, but introduced to Europe, New Zealand, and South America
Known for	"V" formation in migration flight
When	Spring and fall

The migration north in spring takes longer than the trip south. The geese stop often to feed and follow the northward line of melting snow.

Pacific Ocean

Canada

N

United States

Atlantic Ocean

Canada Goose Two-Way Migration Routes

→ Pacific Flyway

→ Central Flyway

→ Mississippi Flyway

→ Atlantic Flyway

Mexico

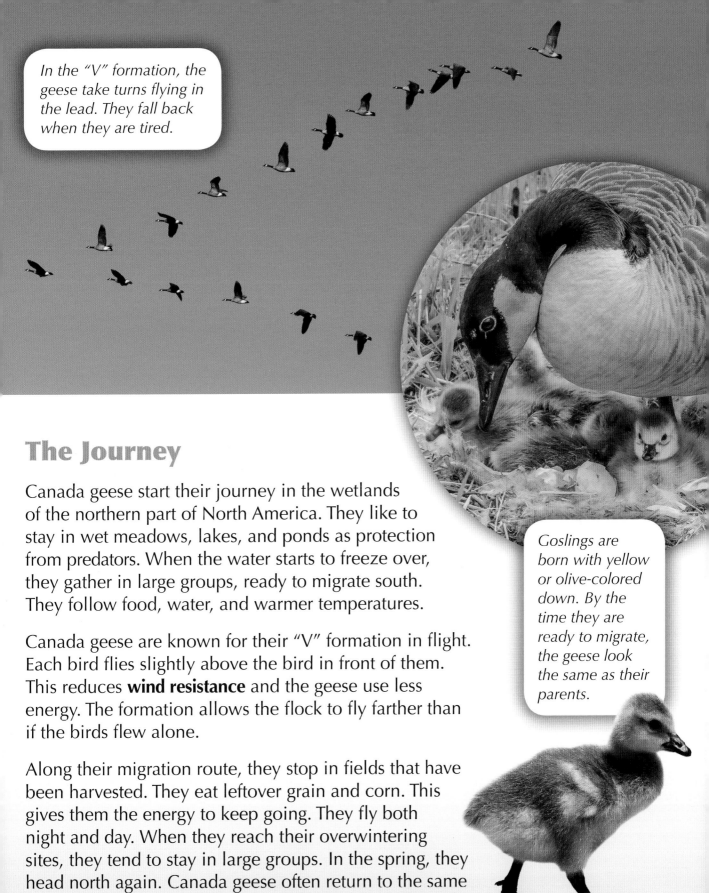

In the "V" formation, the geese take turns flying in the lead. They fall back when they are tired.

The Journey

Canada geese start their journey in the wetlands of the northern part of North America. They like to stay in wet meadows, lakes, and ponds as protection from predators. When the water starts to freeze over, they gather in large groups, ready to migrate south. They follow food, water, and warmer temperatures.

Canada geese are known for their "V" formation in flight. Each bird flies slightly above the bird in front of them. This reduces **wind resistance** and the geese use less energy. The formation allows the flock to fly farther than if the birds flew alone.

Along their migration route, they stop in fields that have been harvested. They eat leftover grain and corn. This gives them the energy to keep going. They fly both night and day. When they reach their overwintering sites, they tend to stay in large groups. In the spring, they head north again. Canada geese often return to the same breeding grounds and even the same nest year after year.

Goslings are born with yellow or olive-colored down. By the time they are ready to migrate, the geese look the same as their parents.

A Special Migration

Geese that are not breeding sometimes leave on a "molt migration" in late May or early June. Molting is a time when birds replace their flight feathers. Geese on a molt migration head to areas north of the breeding grounds. It is easier to spot danger from the open water there. When their new feathers have grown in, they rejoin the breeding geese before the winter migration.

Natural Dangers

It can be exhausting for the geese to fly around 620 miles (1,000 km) a day. When they are tired, they may be less aware of dangers. They are more likely to crash or be killed by predators while on a stopover. If they don't find enough food, they could also die of starvation. Because geese fly and gather in large flocks, diseases spread quickly.

Geese and ducks lose all their flight feathers at the same time, leaving them unable to fly. This makes them vulnerable to predators.

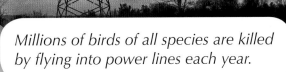

Human Roadblocks

Buildings and power lines are a danger to Canada geese. Chemical poisoning or oil spills are very harmful to migrating birds. If oil from spills gets on their feathers, they cannot fly. Canada geese must also survive hunting season during their fall migration. Even outside official hunting seasons, they are sometimes targeted by illegal hunters or **poachers**. These people hunt them to eat or to stop the birds eating newly planted seeds.

Millions of birds of all species are killed by flying into power lines each year.

Legal Protection

Canada geese are protected by law under the Migratory Birds Convention Act of 1994 in Canada and the Migratory Bird Treaty Act of 1918 in the U.S. Hunters must have a permit and can only hunt the geese during an open season. Bird conservation groups work to protect habitats and breeding grounds.

Geese that have been reintroduced into southern Canada or the northern U.S. may not migrate at all if open water is available year round.

Conclusion

A Vital Journey

Migrations are a vital part of the life cycle of many birds and insects. If migrations are disturbed or made impossible, many animals may die out, plants will not be pollinated, and pests will destroy crops. Many organizations around the world are working to protect migrating animals and their habitats.

Collisions with windows are a big threat for daytime migrating birds. Bird conservation groups encourage people to attach window markers to reduce bird accidents. Organizations such as BirdLife International and FLAP Canada (Fatal Light Awareness Program) suggest that businesses and residences along migration routes turn out their lights inside so as not to attract or confuse nighttime migratory birds.

This is a mark left on a window by a bird flying into it at high speed. Accidents like this can seriously harm birds.

Help Is On the Way

There are ways that everyone can help migratory birds and insects:

- Report sightings of migratory birds with groups such as Whooper Watch to help conservationists keep track of migration route changes or problems.

- Keep your cat indoors. Cats kill millions of birds each year.

- Add window markers to help birds recognize windows and avoid crashing into glass.

- Create bird- and insect-friendly habitats. Migrating insects also need places to stop along their route, with flowers providing nectar and pollen. Planting milkweed will give migrating monarchs a place to lay their eggs for the next generation.

- Avoid using pesticides on your lawns or gardens. These can sicken or kill insects and birds or make them too weak to continue.

- Encourage your family to buy local food and products to reduce **emissions** that contribute to climate change.

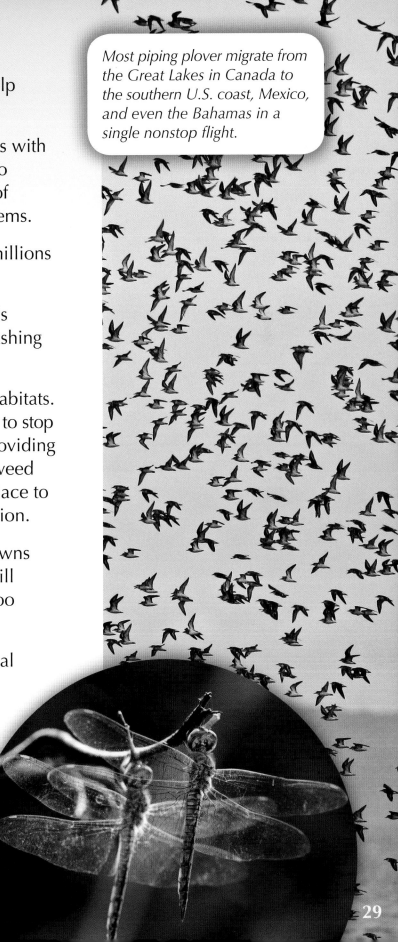

Most piping plover migrate from the Great Lakes in Canada to the southern U.S. coast, Mexico, and even the Bahamas in a single nonstop flight.

At least 11 species of dragonflies are believed to migrate, but scientists are not sure where they come from or go to. Wandering gliders like these are often found in large numbers.

Glossary

beneficial Having good results

camouflage Blending in with your surroundings through color or patterns

climate change Changing weather patterns over time generally considered to be caused by human activity such as fossil fuel use

emissions Gases and chemicals given off by vehicles or factories

generation A group all born and living around the same time

genetic memory A memory that is encoded in your genes

incubators Machines to hatch eggs

larvae A young form of insect that looks like a worm

maternity ward An area for females to give birth and raise their young

pesticides Chemicals used to kill insects on plants

poachers People who kill wild animals illegally

pollinate To fertilize flowers by depositing pollen

predators Animals that hunt other animals for food

reproduce To have babies

roosts Places where birds rest at night

tundra The flat, treeless area in the Arctic

wind resistance The force that you need to move against the air

Find Out More

Books

Bierregaard, Rob. *Belle's Journey: An Osprey Takes Flight*. Charlesbridge, 2018.

Stuckey, Rachel. *Bringing Back the Whooping Crane*. Crabtree Publishing, 2019.

Thornhill, Jan. *Is This Panama?: A Migration Story*. Owlkids, 2013.

Websites

https://bit.ly/2KvwPol
See how other students are creating and caring for monarch butterfly way stations.

www.flap.org/residential_new.php
Learn the best way to prevent bird collisions with your windows.

https://bit.ly/2DPcqow
Be part of Whooper Watch to report on the whooping crane migration.

https://bit.ly/2xUwTUS
Join the Habitat Network to create a migrating insect-friendly garden.

Index